MICROSOFT TEAMS 2020 WITH POWERPOINT NO-FLUFF

Illustrated Microsoft Teams Tips & Tricks for Online Collaboration, Virtual Learning, Online Meetings, Organizational Management and Powerpoint

Leo Kasper

Microsoft Teams 2020 with PowerPoint No-Fluff

Copyright © 2020 Leo Kasper

All rights reserved.

No part of this book may be reproduced, stored in a retrieval system, or transmitted in any form or by any means without the prior written permission of the publisher, except in the case of brief quotations embedded in critical articles or reviews.

Disclaimer:

While every precaution has been taken in the preparation of this book, the publisher assumes no responsibility for errors or omissions, or damages resulting from the use of the information contained herein.

Printed in the United States of America

Table of Contents

CHAPTER ONE 1
- INTRODUCTION 1
- WHAT IS MICROSOFT TEAMS? 1
- FEATURES OF TEAMS 2
- MICROSOFT TEAMS LICENSING REQUIREMENTS 2
- FREE VS PAID VERSION 3
  - How to sign up for a Free Microsoft Teams Version 4
- TEAMS ON WEB OR DESKTOP 5
- MICROSOFT TEAMS INTERFACE 8
- TEAMS INTERFACE FOR TEACHERS 13

CHAPTER TWO 14
- TEAM IN MICROSOFT TEAMS 14
- CREATING NEW TEAM 14
- TEAMS FOR EDUCATIONS AND TRAINING 18
- SETTINGS IN TEAMS 21
- TEAMS MEMBERSHIP 22
  - How to Turn On Guests Access and Invite to Teams 23
  - Creating Team Links 27
  - Modifying Team Membership Status 28
  - How to Change the Name of a Team. 30
  - How to Add or Change a Team Picture. 31
- **CHANNELS IN MICROSOFT TEAMS** 32
  - CREATE CHANNELS IN TEAMS 33

CHAPTER THREE 36

FILE MANAGEMENT IN TEAMS AND CHANNELS 36
TABS IN CHANNELS 36
How to Upload and Edit Files in Channels 37
How to Create a Folder and Upload Files 39
How to Create an Office 365 Files Directly in Channels 43
How to Save Copy of a File in Microsoft Teams 45
How to Create New Tabs 46
COLLABORATING ON FILES 48

CHAPTER FOUR 51

ONLINE MEETINGS AND COLLABORATION 51
SCHEDULING MEETINGS WITHIN TEAMS 58

CHAPTER FIVE 61

ADVANCED TIPS AND TRICKS 61
How to Add Members to Your Team Directly 61
How to Generate Teams Codes 62
How to Use the Status Indicator 64
How to Check the Online Status of all Your Team Members 65
How to Save or Bookmarks Messages 66
How to View Saved Messages 66
How to Translate Teams Messages 68
How to Share Desktop Content in Teams 68
How to View Chat and Hand Raises when Sharing Contents or Presenting in Microsoft Teams 69
How to use Whiteboards in Microsoft Teams 70
How to Track Attendance in Microsoft Teams 70
How to Enable New Features in Microsoft Teams 72

How to use Together Mode 73
How to Check for New Teams Updates 74
Microsoft Teams Keyboard Shortcuts 75

POWERPOINT 77
Presentation Tips and Tricks for Microsoft Teams 77

CHAPTER ONE

INTRODUCTION

In the digital workspace, rules have changed; there is a rise in the use of tools for collaboration, meetings, and chats due to the impact of the global pandemic. Despite all the potentials available in modern workplace technology and software, most organizations are stuck in quite traditional ways of carrying out tasks. Most of these traditional methods of doing things include memo printouts, emails, and physical meetings. Unfortunately, a lot of these meetings have been reduced and done online. Microsoft happens to be a key player in providing applications at a time like this.

This book focuses on Microsoft Teams, one of the best collaboration tools you should learn and start using. It dwells on how to utilize Microsoft Teams, best practices, essential etiquette, as well as tips and tricks to have the best experience with your colleagues.

WHAT IS MICROSOFT TEAMS?

Microsoft Teams is Microsoft's cloud-based application designed to make it easier to carry out collaboration, online meetings, webinars, training, and chats. It is a single hub for work; you can have communication base on persistent chat like on an iMessage on your iPhone or Messenger on an Andriod device. With Microsoft Teams, there can be over 200 people collaborating effectively in a "Teams" meeting. Microsoft Teams works on multiple devices; mobile, web, or desktop.

There are several versions of Microsoft teams available for users; educational, corporate, and the free personal version. The experience on the web is identical to what you get when you make use of the desktop application. Microsoft Teams is more stable and committed to the security of user's data across all devices.

FEATURES OF TEAMS

- Communication through chats like you might have seen with WhatsApp.
- Online Meetings like using Outlook.
- Online Video and Audio call similar to what you have when using a smartphone.
- Office 365 integration, which allows file sharing, data validation, and storage.
- Third-party applications injection to maximize user capabilities.
- Built-in security

MICROSOFT TEAMS LICENSING REQUIREMENTS

There are currently four different Microsoft Teams licenses.

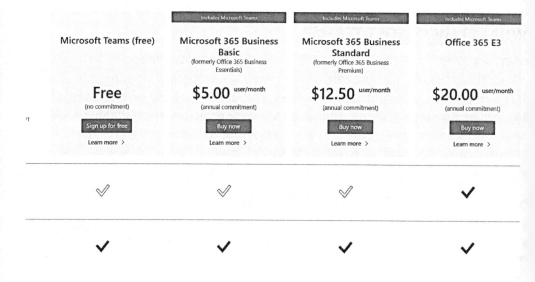

FREE VS PAID VERSION

Features	Free	Paid
Maximum members	500,000 per org	Potentially unlimited with an enterprise license
File storage	2 GB/user and 10 GB of shared storage	1 TB/user
Guest access	Available	Available
1:1 and group online audio and video calls	Available	Available
Channel meetings	Available	Available
Screen sharing	Available	Available
Scheduled meetings	Available	Available
Meeting recording		Available with Microsoft Stream
Phone calls and audio conferencing		Available
Admin tools for managing users and apps		Available
Usage reporting for Microsoft 365 services		Available
99.9% financially-backed SLA uptime		Available
Configurable user settings and policies		Available

How to sign up for a Free Microsoft Teams Version
Small business owners can test run the application with the free version.

To sign up for a Free Version of Microsoft Teams, visit;
https://www.microsoft.com/en-us/microsoft-365/microsoft-teams/free

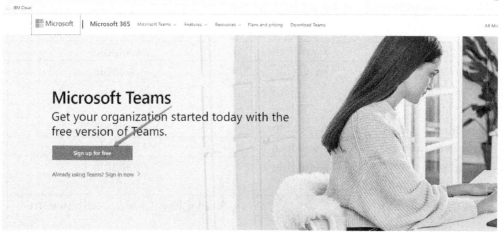

Click on the *Sign up for free* button and follow the onscreen instructions.

TEAMS ON WEB OR DESKTOP

One useful feature of Microsoft Teams is the ability to open the application with your web browser.

So if you are working with different computers, the web browser allows you to jump in and start using Microsoft Teams quickly.
If you are using the desktop app, you don't need to log in every time you start Microsoft Teams on your computer.
There is no much difference between using the web from the desktop app.
You have the option to download Microsoft Teams on your computer or mobile device.

You can also get Microsoft Teams for either Apple or Andriod mobile devices,

Get the Teams mobile app

Enter your phone number or email address and we'll send a download link.

[Send now]

How your phone number or email address is used.

[screenshot of Google Play showing Microsoft Teams "Waiting for download... Verified by Play Protect" with Cancel and Open buttons]

Andriod users can download teams directly from Google Playstore for free.

To install teams on a Mac, on your browser, goto
   www.teams.microsoft.com/downloads

Click on the download button to start the download process. When done, install the application on your Mac system.

MICROSOFT TEAMS INTERFACE

Irrespective of what you are using Microsoft Teams for; education or business, the interface is much more the same. On the left-hand side of your screen is the navigation bar with several menus.

The menus on the navigation bar allow you to access the main parts of Microsoft Teams.

Microsoft Teams Navigation bar

- The *Activity menu* allows you to view all the activities on your Teams app.
- The *Chat menu* is like iMessenger or Whatsapp, where you have your instant messaging. Any messages that you have with a specific team or one in one conversation appears once you click on the chat menu. Chats can be video or text.
- The *Teams Menu* allows you to create your teams and channels
- teams for online learning to give assignments to students or trainees.
- The *Calendar menu* allows you to create schedules, which include an online virtual meeting schedule with team members or private groups.
- The *Calls menu* allows you to make an online call, like making use of your phone to call someone who is on your contact list.
- The *File menu* allows you to share files with members of your Team.

At the bottom of the navigation bar, you have the *Apps menu* that allows you to have access to different apps that you can use to expand the capabilities of Microsoft Teams. The menu with a *Help icon* is used to access fundamental team training topics.

The download menu depending on your interface is used to download the Teams app on your computer. If you already have the Teams app on your computer, you won't see it.

To the right of the navigation bar is the panel area, which describes the current menu you are in.

The panel area allows you to view the teams and channels you have created or teams that you are a member of.

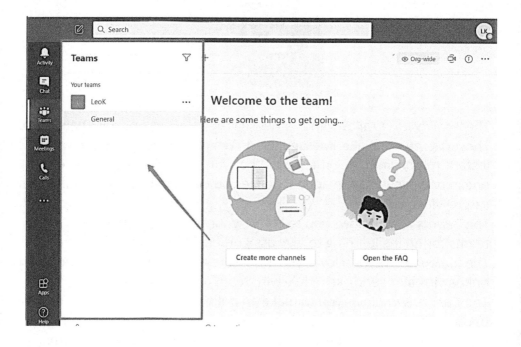

Directly above the panel area is a chat icon.

The chat icon allows you to switch to the chat menu to start chatting. The search bar at the top-mid section of the application allows you to search for a particular keyword.

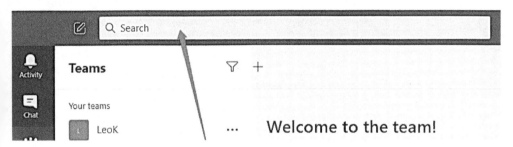

The search bar also functions as your command control center, which allows you to use pre-coded commands like a shortcut to execute a specific task in teams. To use the search bar as a command center, start by entering a slash /, next, you have a list of commands you can use quickly.

On the top-left corner is the user's profile picture icon.

The profile picture icon allows you to carry out basic settings on your user interface. You can click on your profile picture and set the "*Do Not Disturb*" and other settings, which we shall talk about later in this guide.

Below the search bar is the most extensive portion of your Microsoft Teams interface. This portion displays the features of each menu on the navigation bar. When you click on the Teams menu, a list of teams you have created or belong to is displayed.

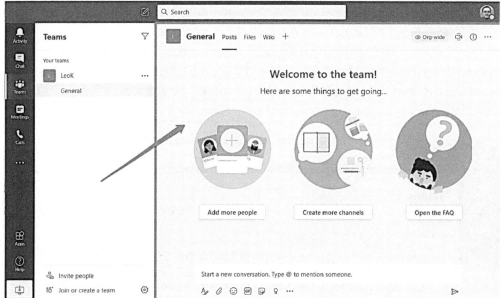

If you go further to click on any existing teams, you will be presented with all the interactions taking place under that particular Team.

Now that you are familiar with the Microsoft Teams Interface, next, we look at what teams and channels are all about and how you can start creating yours.

TEAMS INTERFACE FOR TEACHERS

On the educational version of Microsoft Teams also called *Microsoft Teams for Education*, you have the addition of a Menu called Assignment.

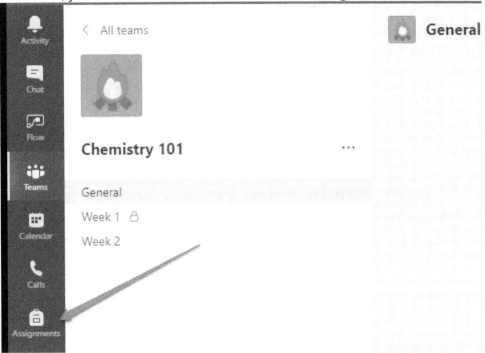

Teachers can use the Assignments menu on the navigation bar to give assignments to students and also assess returned assignments and issue grades.

CHAPTER TWO

TEAM IN MICROSOFT TEAMS

Teams are the primary building blocks of Microsoft Teams for both business and education. Whether you are using Microsoft Teams for education, business, or religious collaboration, the function of Teams is much more the same.

Teams can also be referred to as a book you want to read or a house you want to build. It can be a set of people with relationships, work teams, students, or congregation. As an owner, you can create a team for your working group, your project teams, religious group, or students if you are an educator.

- Businessmen and women create teams for workers, suppliers, or clients.
- Teachers create teams for students, subjects, or co-teachers.
- Religious men and women create teams for workers or congregation.

Whatever teams you create, it must have a specific goal, and that goal must have a relationship with the people you want to add as members. If a new goal is to be created, there is always room to create another team and add only the members needed. Teams can be created as a *Public team* or a *Private team*.

CREATING NEW TEAM

You can create a team for your working group, project, and interest group by clicking on the *Join* or *Create a team* link.

This is also linked to the Teams menu, which gives you access to the *Create team* button.

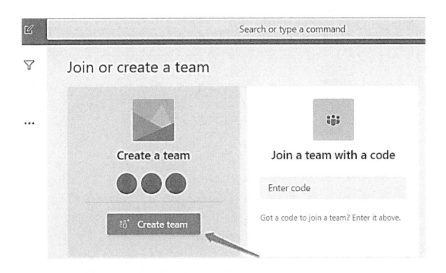

You can build your teams from *scratch* or *extract from an existing team* in office 365.

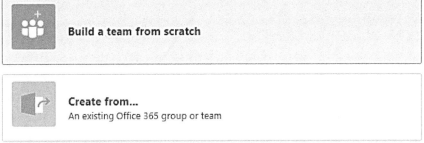

Once you select to *Create a team from scratch*, you can then choose if you want to make it private, and have people ask permission to join.

Give your Team a name and then click on the create button to continue with the process.

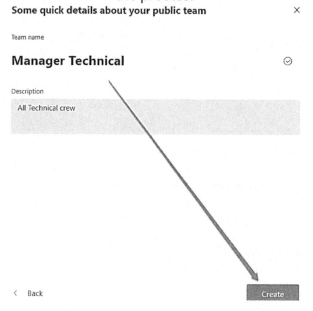

Once you have your Team set up, you will be able to add members.

You are free to add people, groups, or entire contact groups by entering their names or email addresses as guests and then click the *Add* button.

Click on the *skip* button if you wish to ignore to complete the process.

It is advisable to have your teams and channels properly created before adding members for a better user experience.
Your new Team is displayed under the Teams menu.

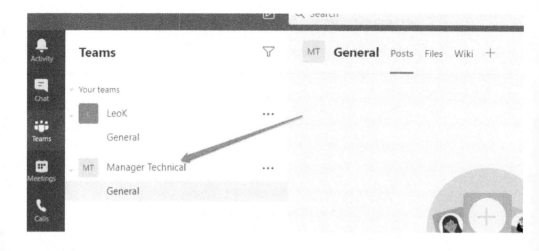

TEAMS FOR EDUCATIONS AND TRAINING

If you are using Microsoft teams for education, the interface is quite the same. Click on the *Create team* button, and next you select the team type you want, which includes; Class, Professional learning community, staff or others

Class teams are meant for you and your students and probably co-teachers. Class teams in Microsoft teams for education enable teachers to give an assignment to students or trainees.
Once you select your choice, you give the Team a name and move on to the next step.

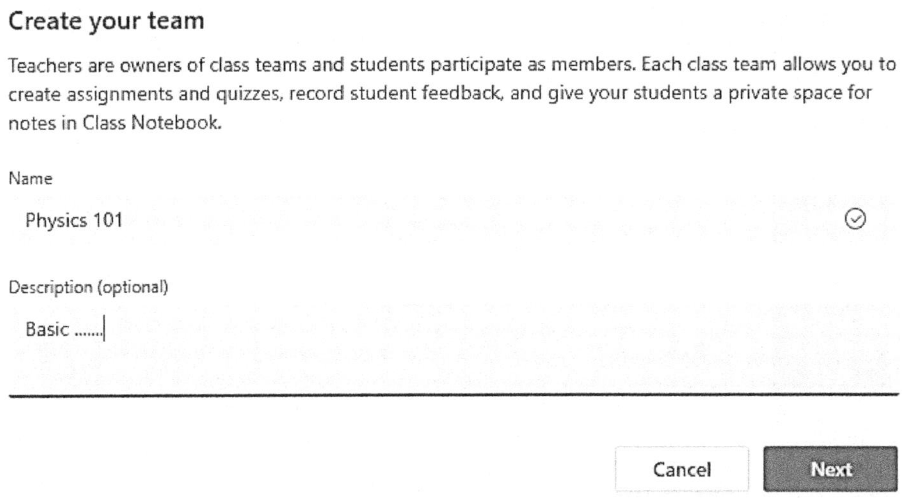

Create your team

Teachers are owners of class teams and students participate as members. Each class team allows you to create assignments and quizzes, record student feedback, and give your students a private space for notes in Class Notebook.

Name

Physics 101

Description (optional)

Basic ....

Cancel   Next

On the next screen, you have the same option as that of the non-educational platform.

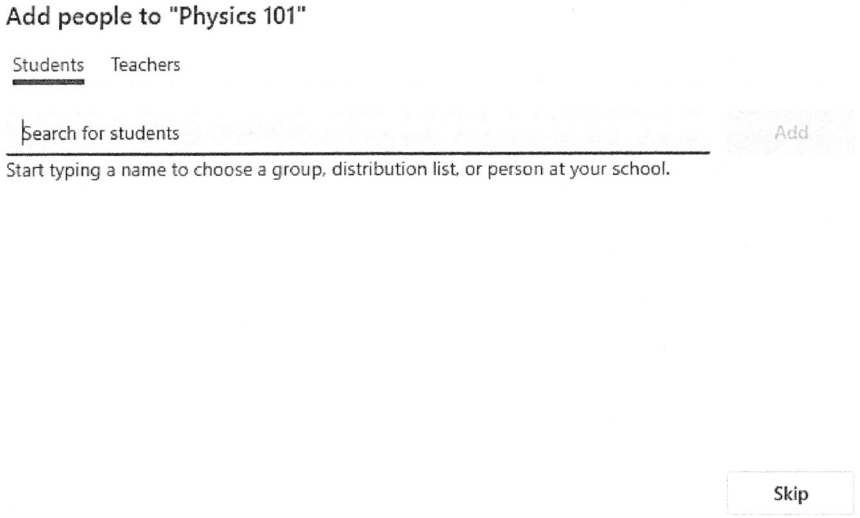

Add people to "Physics 101"

Students   Teachers

Search for students   Add

Start typing a name to choose a group, distribution list, or person at your school.

Skip

Here you can add members, but If you are not ready to add members, click on the skip button to complete the process.

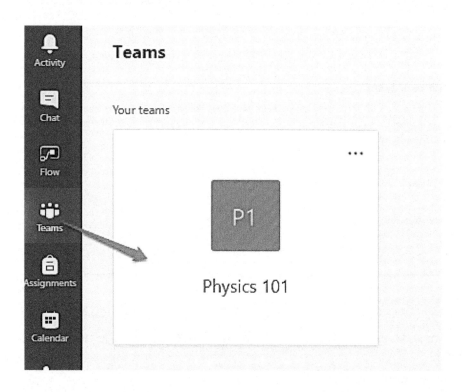

SETTINGS IN TEAMS

There are settings that you can carry out on your teams, such as adding members, changing the Team's icon, or delete a team.
Click on the three-dots beside the Team to have access to these teams settings.

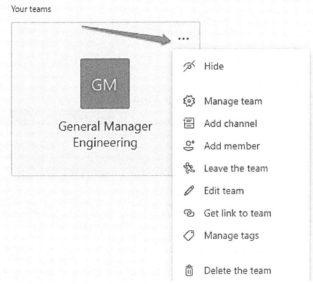

- *Manage team* setting enables you to add or remove members.
- *Add Channel* enables you to create a channel under the Team.
- *Add member* enables you to add members to the Team quickly.
- *Leave the Team* enables you to leave the Team as a member.
- *Edit team* allows you to edit the team features, such as the team icon and name.
- *Get link to Team* enable you to create a link to your Team, which you can share.
- *Manage tags* used to manage tags created in a team
- *Delete the Team* allows you to delete a team.

TEAMS MEMBERSHIP

Click on the three-dots and select Manage teams

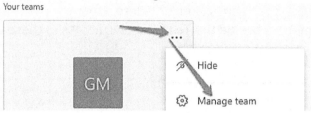

This allows you to see members of your Team.

On the right-hand side of your screen is the *Add member* button. Click on it to add new members.

Another method of adding members is through Teams Codes

How to Turn On Guests Access and Invite to Teams

If you work in a school or an organization and you want your vendors, contractors, or partners to be able to access your Microsoft teams to add their contribution to a conversation and access files or join in a meeting. They can be added as a guest. By default, the guest membership is turned off in Microsoft Teams. You need to turn it on to be able to add guest members to your teams. So click on the *three-dots* near the name of a team and select *Add member*.

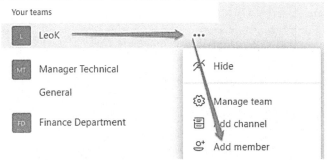

Adding a guest usually starts with an email address

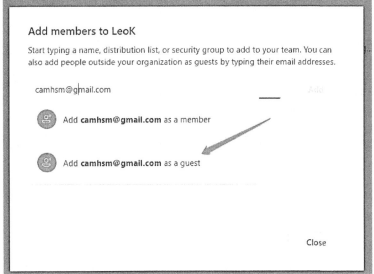

If you are unable to input a guest email address and use the *Add* button, then you need to enable this feature from the Microsoft admin portal.

On your web browser, go to *office.com* and sign in.

When prompted to sign in with your Microsoft admin account, go ahead and sign in. Locate and click on the Admin icon.

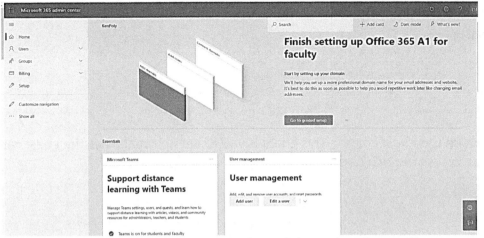

On the Left-hand side is the navigation bar, click on the *Show all* button, and select Teams.

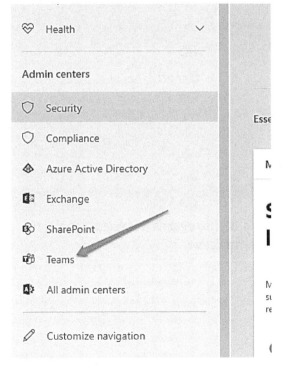

25

On your next screen, click on Org-wide settings and select Guest access.

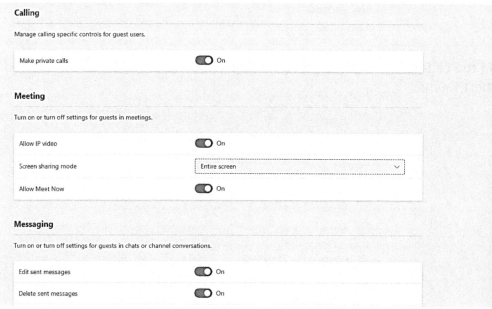

Turn on the *guest* access. This enables you to set up capabilities the guest can have access to, such as calls, meetings, and messaging.

Whatever settings you make as regards the guest capabilities, it takes some time for the changes to become active.

Creating Team Links

When you create a team link, you can share or send through emails asking people to join your Team.

Click on the *Three-dots* beside your Team and select *Get link to Team*.

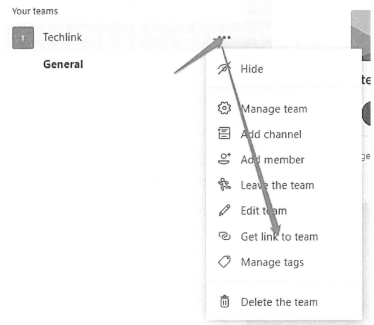

Next, copy the link generated and send or share with people you want to join the Team.

Modifying Team Membership Status

Usually, you can change the membership status of people you are adding to a team right from the process of adding them. When you click on the three-dots near the team name, you have the *Add Member* button.

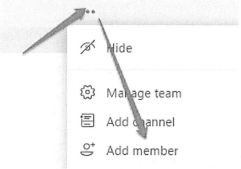

After you are done entering their details, you can change their membership status right before clicking on the close button.

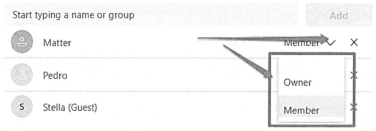

But if you have already added your members and wish to change the status of any of them, click on the *Three-Dots* beside the Teams name and select *Manage team*.

Click on the drop-down arrow on the same row with the member.

Next, select the status you wish to use.

29

How to Change the Name of a Team.

To change your team name and privacy, click on the *Three-dots* beside the Team and select *Edit team*.

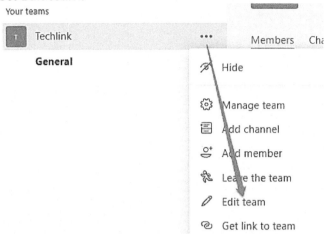

Next, change the name and privacy status.

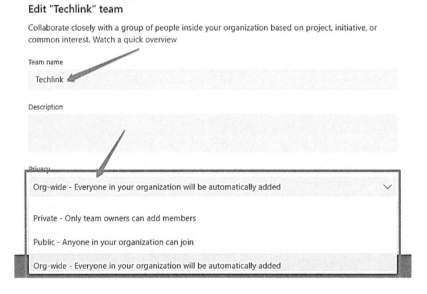

How to Add or Change a Team Picture.

Adding a picture to your Team makes it easy to locate the Team if you have several of them created. It also gives your members an idea of what the Team is all about.
Click on the *Three-dots* beside the Team and select *Manage team*.
Next, click on *Settings* and select T*eam Picture*.

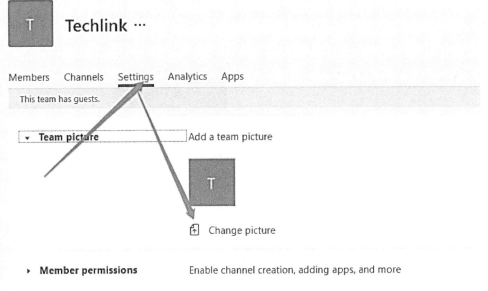

Click on *Change Picture* and upload a picture you want to use.

Click on the *Save* button to complete the process.

CHANNELS IN MICROSOFT TEAMS

Channels are the sub-building blocks in Microsoft Teams. Earlier, we referred to teams as a book or a house. Channels in teams are like the chapters in a book or rooms in a house. Each chapter in a book has a specific goal, so does rooms in a house with separate features.

Channels are dedicated sections within Teams to keep your conversations organized. In an organization, *Channels* can be a specific group of people, topics, or units.

A channel in teams cannot exist on its own without a team.

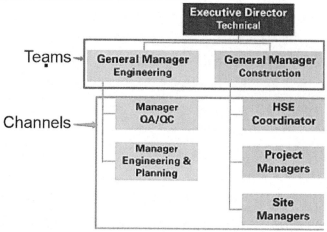

As illustrated above, the Executive Director Technical is a member and owner of the Team *General Manager Engineering* and *General Manager Construction*. Each Team has its channels, private channels can also be created; only members added to such channels can have access to meetings, chats, and collaboration. Furthermore, channels can also be extended using Tabs, Connectors, and Bots.

CREATE CHANNELS IN TEAMS

Immediately a team is created, you have a channel called *General* attached automatically to it by default. The *General Tab* in Teams also has built-in custom tabs to allow you and your team members access services and content in a dedicated space within a channel

The General Tab on Microsoft Teams for Education comes with an additional custom-built tab for *Class Notebook, Assignments, and Grades.*

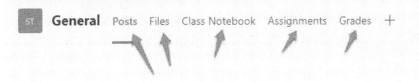

To create a new Channel within a Team,
1. Click on the three-dots near the Team name and select *Add Channel.*

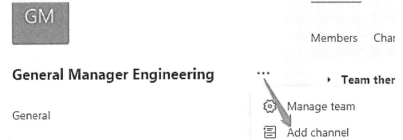

2. Give your Channel a name and choose if you want it standard or private.

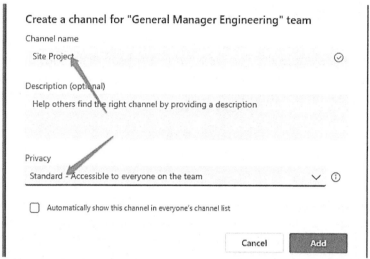

3. Description of the Channel is optional. Click on the checkbox to notify members of the new Channel created. Then click on the *Add* button.

4. Add members to your Channel or skip the process to add them later.

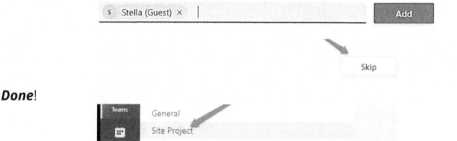

Done!

You can decide to make your Channel public or private. If you make your Channel private, only a few individuals can have access. A private channel can be identified with a padlock sign beside its name.

Create more channels to keep your conversation organized according to specific topics and projects. This way, you can have conversations, share your files, work together on a project, and do more. Your collaboration in channels allows you to bring up a new topic of conversation quickly.

CHAPTER THREE

FILE MANAGEMENT IN TEAMS AND CHANNELS

TABS IN CHANNELS

The General Channel in Teams is the default. However, it can get quickly cluttered with numerous conversations from *Teams* members. Therefore, there is the need to place information and applications you always use in Teams for easy access. Adding more tabs helps you have the applications and information you need at your fingertips. The general *Files tab* should house all files that are stored on your Channel. That said, go into the Files tab and define your folder structure to ensure everything is stored correctly. That means every upload should be stored in the right Folder.

Tabs are created automatically for every Channel you created, and your Team members can get to it quickly on their devices. Usually, you have the post and file tabs created by default.

When you upload your files from your computer to Teams, it goes into the Channel's Files tab you uploaded it to.

The **Posts tab** is pretty much like a chat room, where all the conversation between members of a channel is displayed.

The **File tab** allows you to upload a resource document on your Channel. If you are using a private channel, only selected members can have access to the files related to that Channel.

Files shared in a private or group chat are stored in the owner's OneDrive for Business folder and only accessible to members in that conversation.

How to Upload and Edit Files in Channels

To attach a file in the middle of a conversation, click on the *Paperclip* icon, and select the source of your file.

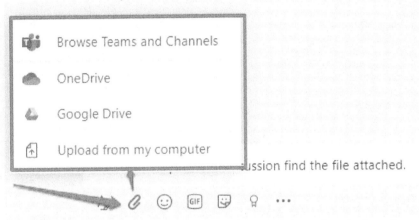

You can attach a file already uploaded to another channel or from your cloud storage, such as Google or OneDrive.

Once the file attachment is complete, you can then click on the *Send* arrow.

The time at which the file and conversation are sent is indicated to confirm it was successful.

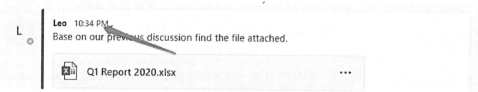

If you wish to delete a conversation and an attachment in a chat, hover around the message and click on the three-dots and select Delete.

But if you wish to edit the attachment. Use the three-dots beside the file name and click on Edit in Teams.

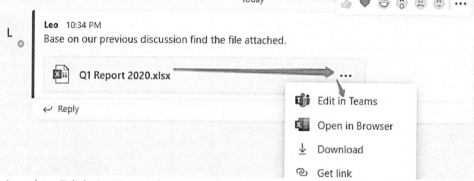

Using the *Edith in Teams* button allows you to use any Office cloud backed services directly in teams. That way, you can open a word or excel files and make modifications directly on the Microsoft teams interface without the need to use the desktop app.

Another option available in uploading files in Channels is through the Files tab. Once you have a file uploaded through the files tab, it is stored in Microsoft SharePoint.

Click on a Channel you want to upload your file and click on the files tab. Next, click on upload.

Next, locate the file on your device or cloud storage.

Under the file tab, you should see the file attached.

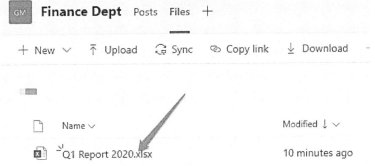

How to Create a Folder and Upload Files

One of the simplest and most overlooked aspects of being organized in Microsoft Teams is getting your files organized. As a teacher or manager of a business, your file list will definitely grow steadily.   Your goal should be able to file easily, find and reuse your uploaded documents in the cloud.

When creating folders in Microsoft Teams, let it be minimal as much as possible. Files and folders should be named strategically.
With Microsoft Teams, your files can be stored in your OneDrive or Google Drive. This is also applicable to Microsoft Teams for Education.

To create a Folder in Teams, click on the Files tab in the Channel you want to use.

Next, click on the arrow pointing downwards new the *New menu.*

Next, click on Folder

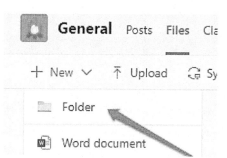

Enter the name for your new Folder without special characters.

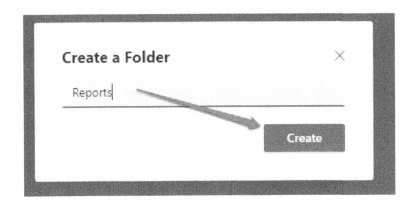

Click on the Create button when done.

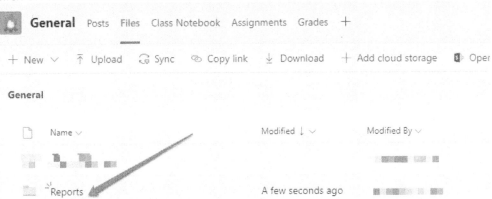

To upload a file into your Folder, click on the folder name to open it.
Next, use the upload menu to search for your file and upload it into the Folder you just created.

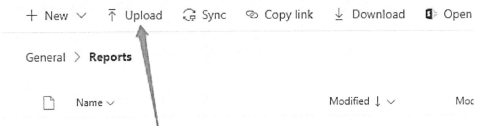

To Delete a file you mistakenly uploaded, go beside the file name and click on the circle to highlight the file.

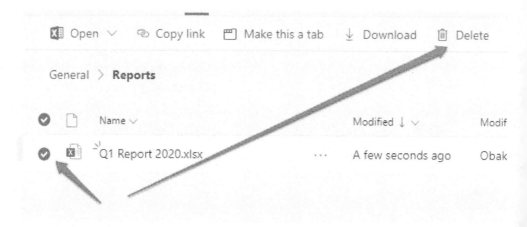

Next, click on the Delete menu to remove the file.

How to Create an Office 365 Files Directly in Channels

You can quickly create a new file in Microsoft Teams using office 365 capabilities. This way, you can create either a Word, Excel, Powerpoint, or Onenote Notebook directly on the Microsoft Teams interface.

Under the file tab in your Channel, click on **New**

Select for the list the type of tile you want to create.

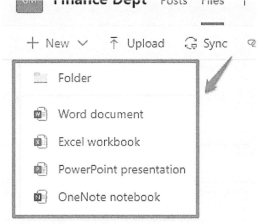

Give the new file a name, and click on the *create* button.

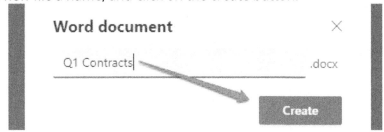

Wait for the interface to be prepared for you to start entering your information.

For a word document, you have an interface similar to your Microsoft Word application.

If you have a Word app already installed on your device, click on *Open in Desktop app.*

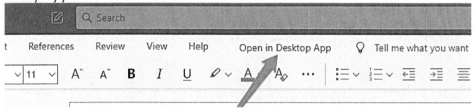

How to Save Copy of a File in Microsoft Teams

To download a copy of your files attached to Microsoft Teams, click on the *File* to edit it. This will open the file in the cloud-based service platform.

Next, use the File > *Save AS* menu and select your option.

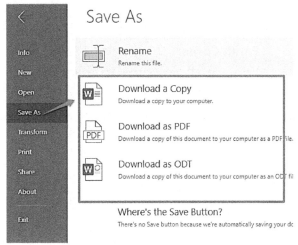

- Download a copy create and copy of the original file and save the duplicate in your computer
- Download as PDF converts the duplicate into a PDF and saves it on your computer.
- Download as ODT creates a duplicate and saves in your computer as an Office Deployment Tool.

45

How to Create New Tabs

For convenience, you need a new tab for mostly used files, applications, or web pages by your team members. Any files that might become referential should have their tabs. Before converting a File to a tab, you must have uploaded the file in a Channel.

To add new tabs to the existing tabs created by default in a channel, click on the plus icon.

From the list of options provided, make your selection base on the nature of the tab.

As illustrated above, if it is an excel file uploaded in a different channel you want to make as a tab, click on the Excel icon to narrow your search to all spreadsheet files .

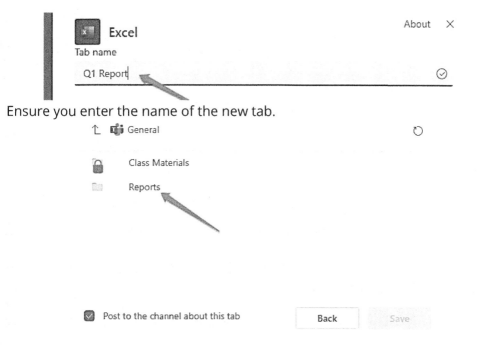

Ensure you enter the name of the new tab.

Teams allow you to search for such files. So, select the file and click on the Save Button.

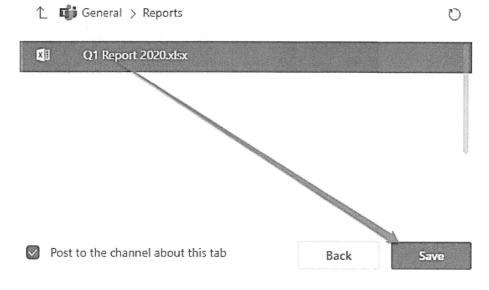

Your new tab is placed beside the previous last tab.

To Move a tab to any position, click and drag to where you want it to appear. But it can not be placed before the default tabs.

COLLABORATING ON FILES

As a member of a team, you can carry out collaboration with other team members on a single project file.

To access your team's shared files, click the Files tab.

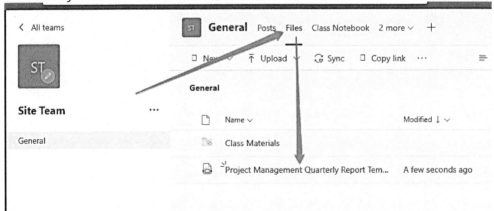

Next, click on a file to open a preview.

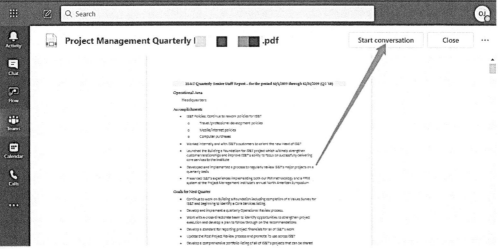

The file preview opens a read-only, so to use the document for a conversation, click the "Start Conversation" button.

On the left of your screen appear a chat section to use for your document collaboration.

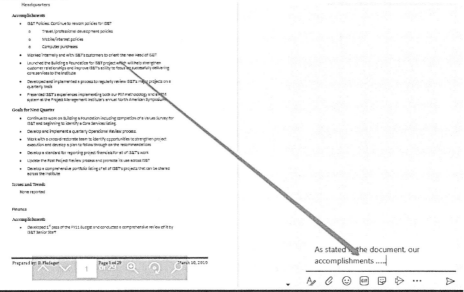

Use the arrow icon to send your message when done.

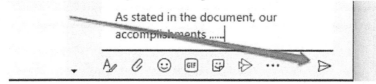

All the collaboration between you and your team members will be displayed on the left panel of your screen.

CHAPTER FOUR

ONLINE MEETINGS AND COLLABORATION

Meetings can be scheduled within a channel in Teams. You can also start an instant meeting by clicking on the small camera icon in any of your Team's channels or in the Meeting menu.

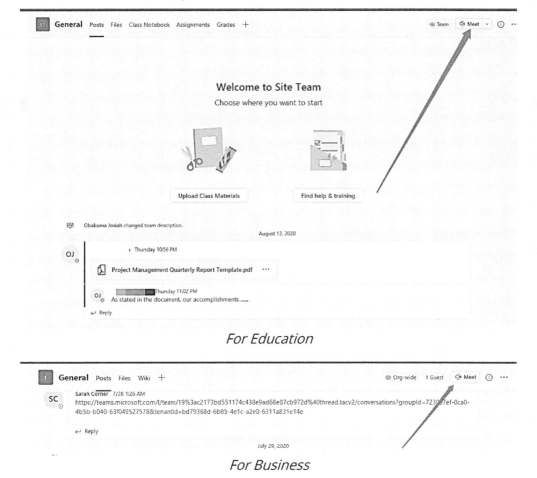

For Education

For Business

When you click on the meeting menu, you have two options to choose from regarding meetings.

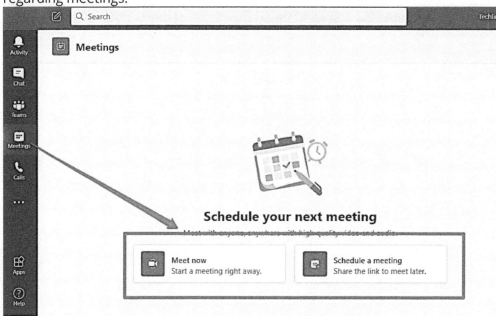

You either use the **_Meet now_** option or **_Schedule a meeting_**.

Irrespective of the version of Microsoft Teams you are using, the *Meet* icon starts an online meeting instantly with sound and video. You can access the *Meet* button at the left corner of any Channel.

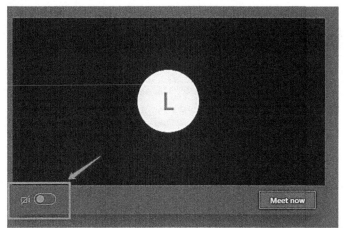

On the next screen, you have the option to give your meeting a *Subject* (Topic), turn on or off your microphone and camera before joining the meeting finally.

Click on the *Meet* button to join or start the meeting.

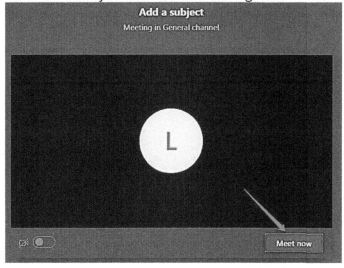

While in a meeting, you can also invite people to join by clicking on the Show participants button.

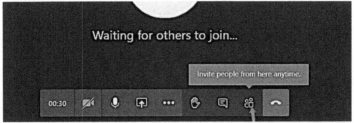

Upon clicking on the *Show Participant* button, you will have displayed on the right side of your screen the *People* panel, where you can enter the names or emails of participants to send an invitation to join your meeting online.

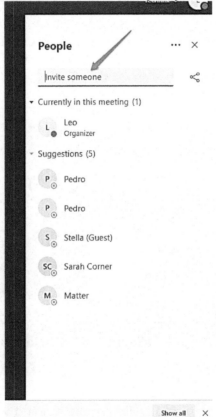

Once participants join your meeting, you will see their names in bold ink. If they are yet to accept the invitation, their names will look faded.

To manage permissions such as who can speak or share their screen during a meeting, click on the three-dots in the *People* panel and select manage permissions.

People — ✗ Manage permissions / Download attendance list

Leo — Organizer

Suggestions (5)

Pedro

Here you have the option to carry out settings regarding your participants.

Furthermore, other buttons available for your meetings control includes;
- **The timer** button indicates how long you have stayed on the meeting from the time you joined the meeting.

The timer automatically resets once your hangup or gets disconnected from a meeting.

- **The Camera** button allows you to toggle on or off the camera on your device. If you don't have a camera connected to your computer, this icon will appear with a slash.

- ***The Mute*** button allows you to toggle on or off the microphone on your device.

- ***The ScreenSharing*** button allows you to share your device screen with participants in an online meeting.

- ***The Mute*** button allows you to turn OFF or ON your microphone

- ***The Camera*** button allows you to turn OFF or ON your Webcam or external camera.

- ***The Timer*** button indicates how long you have stayed connected to an online meeting.

With the latest version of Microsoft Teams, a popup appears on your screen once you are connected to a meeting successfully. You have the option to quickly copy your meeting link and share or invite people via their email.

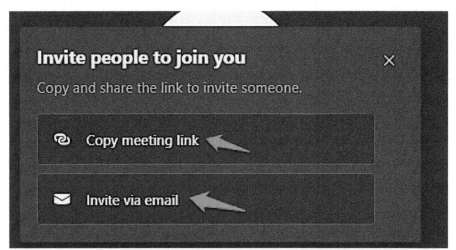

To hang up an online meeting, click on *the **hang-up*** botton to disconnect.

SCHEDULING MEETINGS WITHIN TEAMS

To schedule a meeting in Microsoft Teams, click on the Meeting menu.

Once you click on the Schedule a Meeting button, you will need to enter the title and period when the meeting is to start.

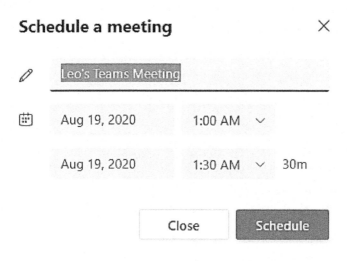

When done, you click on the *Schedule* button.

Next, you have the option to copy the meeting invitation or share the invitation you're your Google calendar.

If you are using Microsoft Teams for Education, the schedule meeting feature is found under the Calendar menu.

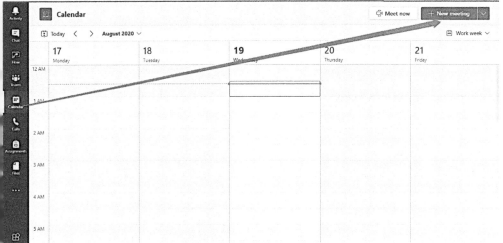

In this case, it is referred to as **New meeting**.

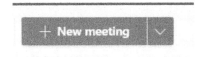

Next, set up the Meeting details, using all the available data required.

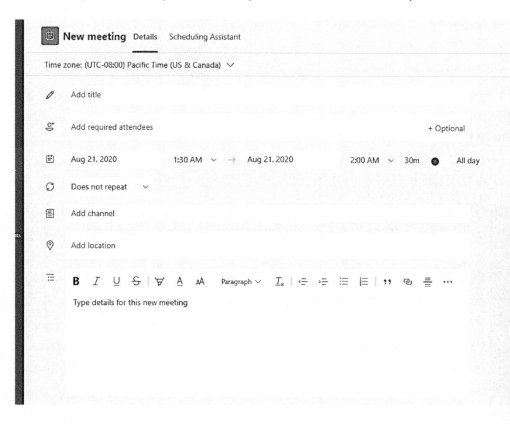

CHAPTER FIVE

ADVANCED TIPS AND TRICKS

How to Add Members to Your Team Directly.

If you skipped adding members to your Team when creating it, you could still do so by clicking on the three-dots and select add members.

Such members must be within your organization's contact list, to be able to search for their detail such as name or email address to add them to a team.

How to Generate Teams Codes

Teams codes is a fast means of adding members to your Team. It only involves generating a code which you mail to people to join a team. To do this, go to the manage team settings.

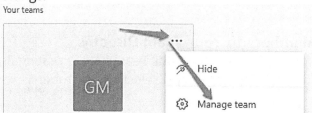

Next, click on the *Settings* tab.

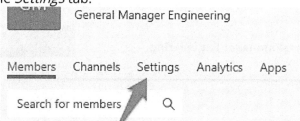

Click on Team code.

Member permissions	Enable channel creation, adding apps, and more
Guest permissions	Enable channel creation
@mentions	Choose who can use @team and @channel mentions
Team code	Share this code so people can join the team directly - you won't get join requests

Click on the *Generate* button.

Next, copy the code generated and send as a mail to people you cant to join the Team.

People who received the mail or the code can join your Team by using the *Join or Create team* option after clicking on the Team menu.

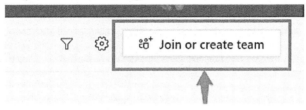

Next, the person enters the code and clicks the *Join team* button.

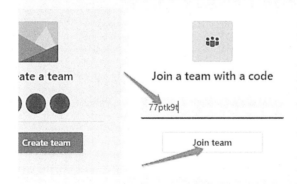

How to Use the Status Indicator

Microsoft Teams has indicators on the desktop, the web, iOS, and Android, which alert you to the existence of the people you are collaborating with.

Irrespective of where you are using Microsoft Teams to work from work and communicate with your team, your online presence very important. Your ability to know when a client is online can be crucial to business operations. You don't want to send a message without your clients available online to see it.

Teams have various online presence indicators, and are set by clicking your profile picture and then choosing one of the status indicators.

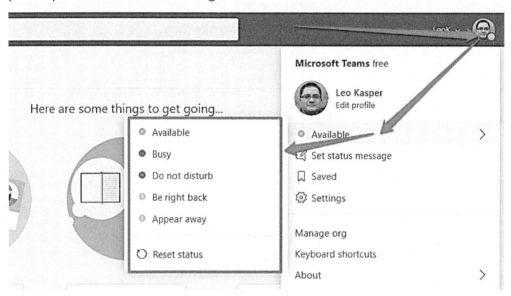

Your status is set automatically by Teams, so when you come online, you have the online screen status. Then, when you are active or not using the app for a few minutes, you have the away status. Additionally, if you are making a call, you have an inactive or busy status to let your team members know you aren't available.

How to Check the Online Status of all Your Team Members

There are various ways to check a specific team member's online presence. However, one familiar and quite comfortable way of checking the online presence of all your team members at once is through the Manage team settings.

Click on the team name, click on the three dots, and then select Manage team.

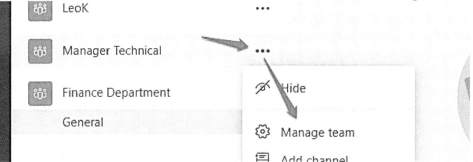

Every member of your team that is online right at that moment has the green circle with a checkmark next to their name.

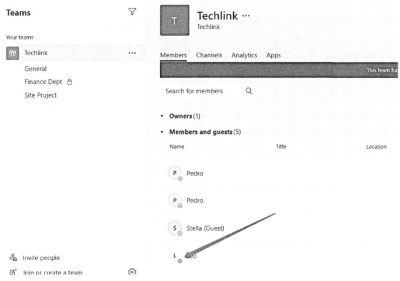

How to Save or Bookmarks Messages
This functionality allows you to save a specific message in a conversation or chat by clicking on the three dots '...' menu next to the message.

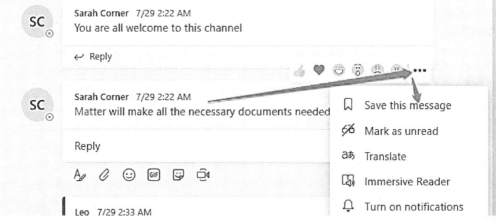

How to View Saved Messages
To recall all your saved messages, click on your profile picture and select 'Saved'.

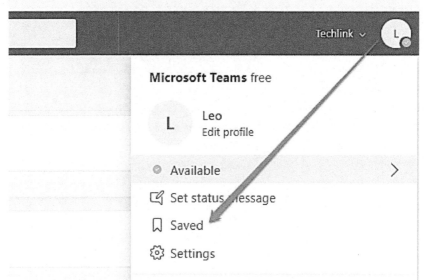

Alternatively, type in the command bar /saved

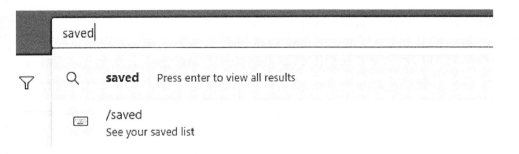

Press the enter key to view all your saved messages.

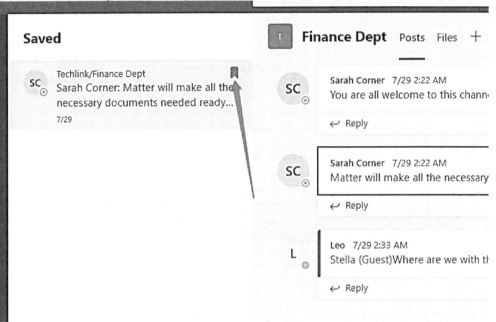

How to Translate Teams Messages

You can translate messages to your preferred language in Microsoft Teams. To do this, click on the three dots beside the message you want to translate and choose translate.

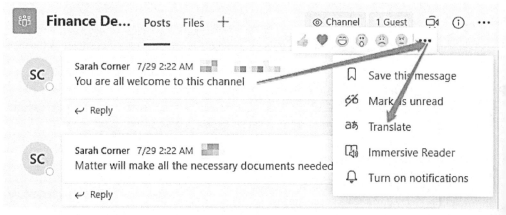

How to Share Desktop Content in Teams

To share content during a meeting in Microsoft Teams, move your mouse or pointer to the meeting controls and click on the share content button.

This opens up all the different content sharing options available in Microsoft Teams at the bottom of your screen.
Next, locate Desktop among the options and click on it.

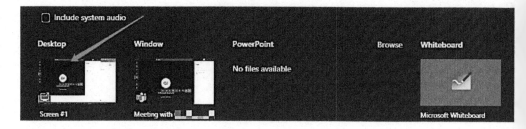

How to View Chat and Hand Raises when Sharing Contents or Presenting in Microsoft Teams

As a presenter in a meeting, your audience might like to raise their hands to ask questions.

Usually, when you share your desktop, you won't see chats and when people raise hands to ask questions or seek your attention. This may force you to toggle between your desktop and teams meeting window.

To solve this problem, slipt your screen and have your presentation on one side, while the other part of the screen accommodates the Teams Windows as illustrated below.

Another way is to login to your Microsoft Teams account on two devices. Log into your account using your laptop and your mobile device simultaneously.

That way, you can use the laptop for sharing your content, while the mobile device is used to view participants' reactions such are raised hands. Practically, your phone or any mobile device serves as your second screen.

How to use Whiteboards in Microsoft Teams

Whiteboards are useful when running virtual meetings and can do more things than a traditional whiteboard. To use a whiteboard in Microsoft teams requires sharing your screen.

When you click on the share content button, you will be presented with options to choose from, including a whiteboard.

The Microsoft whiteboard has limited features, but you can also download and used the Microsoft Whiteboard App.

How to Track Attendance in Microsoft Teams

Tracking attendance is crucial in Microsoft Teams to have a record of your meeting participants. It is useful for both educators and at workplaces. To be able to track attendance in Microsoft teams, you have to be a meeting organizer. However, the admin has to enable this feature in teams to allow you to download attendance reports.

First, you start your meeting, and when it is time to track the attendance, click on the *Show Participants button*.

Next, on the Participant or People panel, click on the arrow pointing downwards to download the attendance list.

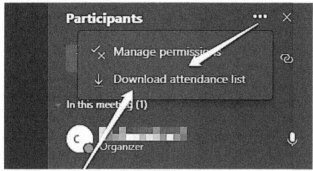

Once you click on the download attendance list button, give teams some time to download the file. Locate the file in your download folder and open the *.CSV file* using a spreadsheet application.

In the attendance list, you will see the name of the participant, time when they joined the meeting, and when they left.

How to Enable New Features in Microsoft Teams

Click on the picture or profile icon and click on *Settings*.

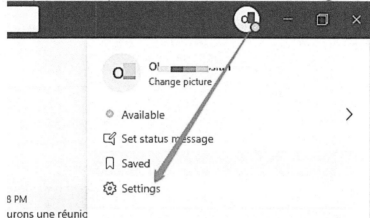

Next, under the general tab, scroll down and click on *Turn on new meeting experience (New meetings and calls will open in separate windows. Requires restarting Teams.)*

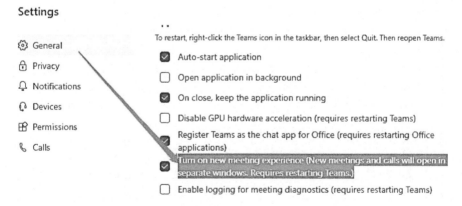

Once done, teams will need a restart to make the charges.

How to use Together Mode

Together mode is a new feature in teams that makes your meetings more realistic, making all participants feel more together.

While in a meeting, locate the 3-dots on the control tab and click on it.

Next, click on *Together mode*.

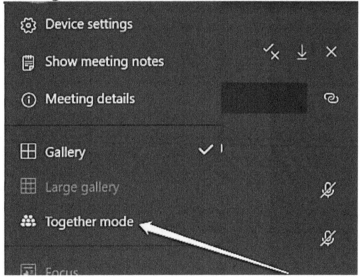

How to Check for New Teams Updates

If you are not always online and wish to check for new Microsoft teams updates for your desktop application, click on the Profile picture icon and select *Check for Updates.*

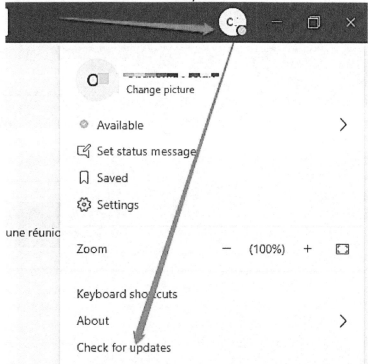

This will carry out a background update while you are still using teams. You won't be asked to close the application; rather the available updates will be done in the background.

Microsoft Teams Keyboard Shortcuts

General

Show keyboard shortcuts	**Ctrl .**
Show commands	**Ctrl /**
Goto	**Ctrl Shift G**
Start new chat	**Alt N**
Open Help	**Ctrl F1**
Go to Search	**CtrlE**
Open filter	**Ctrl Shift F**
Open apps flyout	**Ctrl `**
Open Settings	**Ctrl Shift ,**
Close	**Escape**

Navigation

Open Activity	**Ctrl Shift 1**
Open Teams	**Ctrl Shift 3**
Open Files	**Ctrl Shift 5**
Go to previous list item	**Alt ↑**
Go to previous section	**Ctrl Shift F6**
Open Chat	**Ctrl Shift 2**
Open Calls	**Ctrl Shift 4**
Open Files	**Ctrl Shift 6**
Go to next list item	**Alt ↓**
Go to next section	**Ctrl F6**

Messaging

Go to compose box	**Alt Shift C**
Expand compose box	**Ctrl Shift X**
Attach file	**Ctrl Shift O**
Search current Chat/Channel messages	**Ctrl F**
Reply to thread	**AltShiftR**
Send (expanded compose box)	**CtrlEnter**
Start new line	**Shift Enter**

Meetings, Calls, and Calendar

Accept video call	**Ctrl Shift A**
Decline call	**Ctrl Shift D**
Start video call	**Ctrl Shift U**
Go to sharing toolbar	**Ctrl Shift Space**
Go to current time	**Alt.**
Go to next day/week	**Ctrl Alt →**
View workweek	**Ctrl Alt 2**
Save/send meeting request	**Ctrl S**
Go to suggested time	**Alt Shift S**
Accept audio call	**Ctrl Shift S**
Start audio call	**Ctrl Shift C**
Toggle mute	**Ctrl Shift M**
Schedule a meeting	**Alt Shift N**
Go to previous day/week	**Ctrl Alt ←**
View day	**Ctrl Alt 1**
View week	**Ctrl Alt 3**
Join from meeting details	**Alt Shift J**

POWERPOINT
Presentation Tips and Tricks for Microsoft Teams
Microsoft Powerpoint is part of the Microsoft Office 365 suite that generally uses a graphic approach to present content using text boxes and images. The use of graphics in Powerpoint is much flexible than that of applications like Photoshop. When you start a meeting in Microsoft Teams, you have the control buttons. To share your already open PowerPoint presentation, you click on the share button.

Next, you are presented with options to choose from, among which is the *Desktop*.

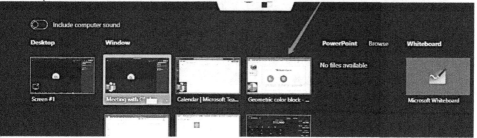

If you click on *Desktop,* you will be able to share your entire screen displaying the applications you are currently using. The challenge however, with sharing your *Desktop* is that you can't view the chat or the participant's panel anymore.

To be sure and focus on a particular Powerpoint file you wish to share, click on the Browse button and search for the file.

Next, upload the Powerpoint file from your computer or OneDrive.

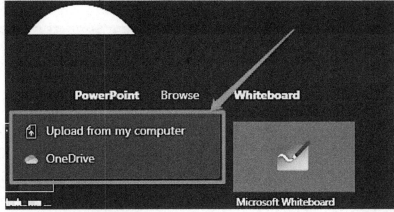

Locate the file, click on it and then click on the *Open* button to start the upload process

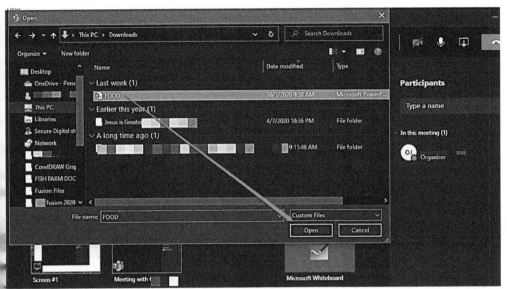

Files you uploaded or shared with participants will be stored automatically in your OneDrive. That way, you can go back to use it later.

Once loaded, you will see the chat panel on the right side of your screen to view the reactions of your participants.

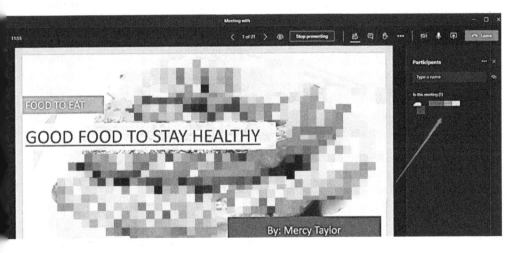

With the updated version of Microsoft Teams, you will have your number of slides displayed on the top.

The right and left arrows allow you to move to your previous or next slide.

Shared slides can be moved through by your participants. To prevent participants from moving through your shared slide, and have full control of what they can see, click on the *Eye icon*.

This way, only the presenter can move to the next slide during a presentation. To stop your presentation, click on the *Stop presenting* button.

When you want to share the Powerpoint file, you previously uploaded from your computer, click on *Browse* and select *OneDrive*. A copy of your previous presentations shared will is stored in *OneDrive* automatically.

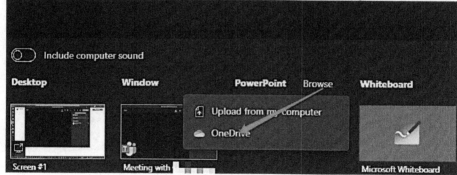

Click on Microsoft Teams Chat Files folder to view your previously shared files

To prevent participants from sending messages using a presentation that might distract you, click on the Profile picture and change your status to *Do not disturb*.

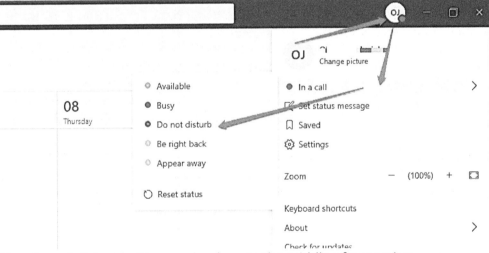

The *Do not disturb* setting can be done in the middle of a meeting.

How to use Powerpoint Presenter View in Microsoft Teams

Suppose you are having difficulty in going into the PowerPoint presenter view when sharing a presentation. Teams give way too many choices as to what to present, and if you don't choose the right one, you won't have access to the presenter's view. Additionally, when your work schedule does not give you adequate time to do your job, it creates an even bigger struggle.

There are a couple of things you need to put in place;
1. Create a side note to help you cover all the key points on each slide. Note also help you know what is coming up in the next slide to avoid fluster.
2. The presenter view also makes your presentation more dynamic with annotation tools made available to use.
3. Before you start the meeting, run a test view of the presentation to see how it looks at the attendee's perspective.

So to share your presentation, **ensure** the PowerPoint application is **running** and the file open and ready.

When you start your meeting, click on the share content button

And from the options made available, ensure you select the PowerPoint presentation window.

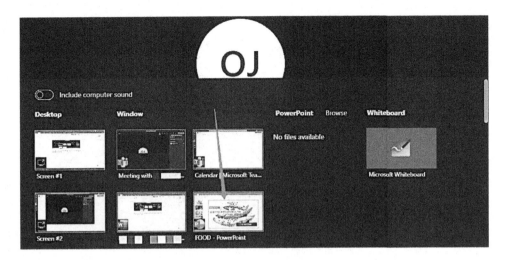

Notice this time; the **Browse** button was not used.

Next on your screen will be your PowerPoint presentation window, displaying the entire application window.

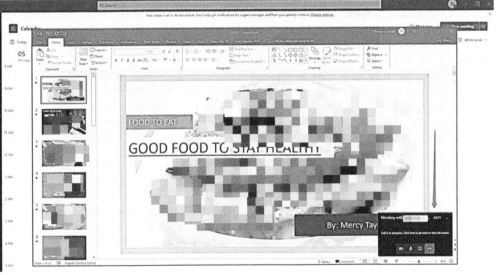

The meeting window floats the Powerpoint window, with a docked area to enable you to stop the screen sharing or to stop the meeting immediately.

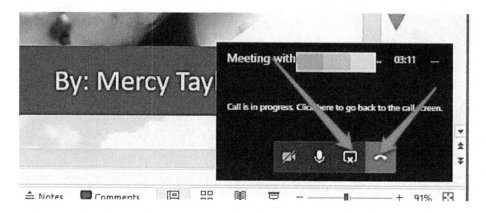

Meanwhile, during this process, your entire Powerpoint Windows is visible to your participants. So immediately, you need to click on the *Slide Show* button located at the bottom right corner of your screen to start the presentation

or press **F5** function key. This will display just the current slide on your screen.

To activate the Presenter View, right-click your mouse on the current slide and select *Show Presenter View*.

The presenter view displays what your attendees can view in the larger box, and the Next slide.

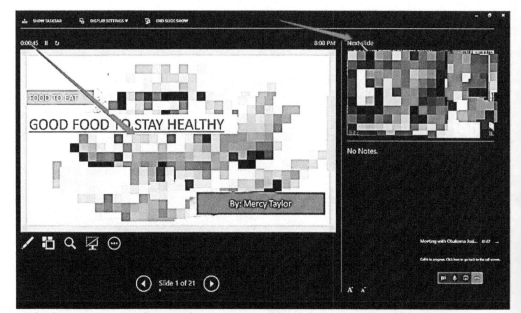

Only the slide in the largest box is viewed at a time by your attendees.
The Next slide box, gives you the presenter, an idea of what the next slide looks like so you don't get caught off guard.

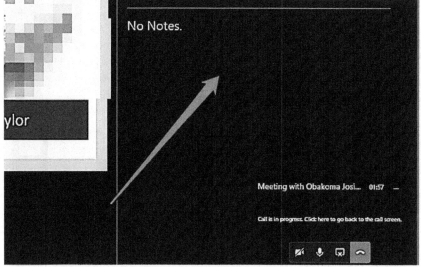

The Note area is where you drop notes or key points during a presentation.

You also have control tools to use while presenting.

The **Laser tool** is like your pointer to focus on a particular spot on your slide. With this button, you can change the color of the pointer and highlighter.

The **See all Slide** button allows you to view your slide sorter at once.

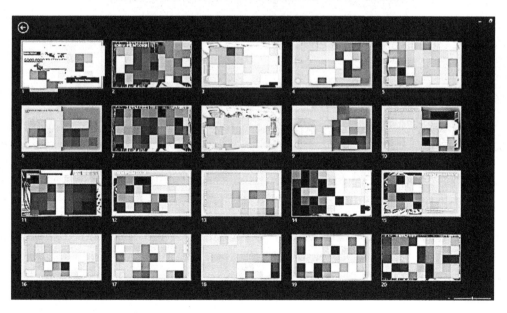

The **zoom into Slide** is a tool you use to zoom in to a particular spot on your slide during a presentation. It magnifies the size of the area.

The **Blank or unblank Slide** tool is used to turn the current slide blank. May be used when you want to turn off the slide but not stop the presentation.

The **More slide show options** tool gives you additional features to use, including turning off the Presenter View.

Note when carrying out a presentation using the presenter view, only the larger boxed area is visible to the participants.

Another way to quickly activate the Presenter View once you share the Powerpoint Window is to press **Alt F5** as soon as you share the Powerpoint Window. A combination of these two keys immediately drops you in the presenter's view.

Best Shortcut Keys During a Presentation

Using shortcut keys while presenting is much more effective when presenting online

F5 – Jump into your presentation

W – turns your screen bright white, hiding the content of the current slide and makes your attendees focus on you.

B - turns your screen black, hiding the content of the current slide and makes your attendees focus on you.

To jump to a particular slide, press the slide number and then thhe Enter key.

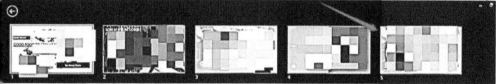

So if I want to jump to slide number 5, I press **5** then the **Enter** key.
f you can't remember a particular slide you want to jump to, press **Ctrl S** to
oring up the list.

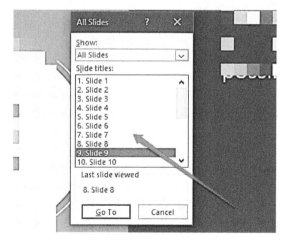

Ctrl P-	To activate Pen for annotation.
E -	To erase any annotation
Ctrl I-	To activate highlighter.
Ctrl A-	To activate arrow.
Ctrl L-	To activate laser pointer.
+ or -	To zoom in or zoom out while using your mouse pointer to pin around your screen.
J -	To turn on subtitles from translation
Ctrl H-	To hide mouse cursor.
Ctrl A-	To unhide mouse cursor.
Ctrl U-	Also to unhide mouse cursor.
ESC-	Ends presentation